Thomas
Edison

Other titles in the Inventors and Creators series include:

Benjamin Franklin
Dr. Seuss
Henry Ford
Jim Henson
Jonas Salk

Inventors and Creators

Thomas
Edison

Sheila Wyborny

KIDHAVEN PRESS

THOMSON
™
GALE

Detroit • New York • San Diego • San Francisco
Boston • New Haven, Conn. • Waterville, Maine
London • Munich

On cover: Edison in his lab.

Library of Congress Cataloging-in-Publication Data

Wyborny, Sheila, 1950–
  Thomas Edison / by Sheila Wyborny
    p. cm. — (Inventors and creators)
  Includes bibliographical references and index.
  Summary: Discusses the life of Thomas Edison, including his early
  childhood, education, interests, and inventions.
  ISBN 0-7377-0994-4 (hardback : alk. paper)
    1. Edison, Thomas A. (Thomas Alva), 1847–1931—Juvenile
  literature. 2. Inventors—United States—Biography—Juvenile
  literature. 3. Electrical engineers—United States—Biography—
  Juvenile literature. [1. Edison, Thomas A. (Thomas Alva),
  1847–1931. 2. Inventors.] I. Title. II. Series.
  TK140.E3 W59 2002
  621.3'092—dc21

2001007831

Copyright 2002 by KidHaven Press,
an imprint of The Gale Group
10911 Technology Place, San Diego, CA 92127

Contents

An Inventor of Necessities

Thomas Alva Edison is one of America's greatest and best-known inventors. Edison's inventions dramatically changed the way people lived.

Although Edison had little education, he liked to learn; he wanted to know how machines worked. He also wanted to understand why things in nature, such as bees in beehives, acted the way they did. He spent much of his childhood observing, experimenting, and building models.

As a young man, Edison was often fired from jobs for not paying enough attention to his work. Instead, he performed experiments on company time, and sometimes these experiments damaged his employers' property.

When Edison was able to focus all of his time and energy on inventing, he created many things that we consider necessities today, such as electric lights and telephone systems. He also was able to develop new ways of listening to music and motion pictures.

Thomas Edison turned thousands of ideas into useful inventions.

During his years at Menlo Park, New Jersey, the world's first "invention factory," and later at his second facility in West Orange, New Jersey, Edison and his team of scientists and engineers developed more than one thousand inventions.

Chapter One

Curious Al

Thomas Alva Edison was born on February 11, 1847, in Milan, Ohio. He was the youngest of seven children and was nicknamed "Al" by the family. Three of the Edison children died before he was born, so by the time Thomas came along his brother and sisters were already teenagers. His father, Samuel Edison Jr., worked at many different kinds of jobs, and Thomas's mother, Nancy Elliot Edison, was a teacher.

Curiosity and Consequences

Early on, his parents saw that young Thomas was a curious child. Sometimes his curiosity led him into trouble. Once, he wanted to know if a person could hatch eggs, so he sat on a chicken's nest. Of course he crushed all of the eggs. Another time, Thomas wanted to see how grain was stored. He climbed the side of the grain elevator and fell in. He sunk into the grain over his head and nearly died because he could not breathe. But the time his curiosity got him into the most trouble was when he was six and he set fire to his father's barn. He wanted to see what fire would do. As punishment, his father spanked him in front of the entire neighborhood.

When he was seven years old, Thomas's family moved to Port Huron, Michigan, and he started school. Although Thomas was smart, he did not get along well in

Young Thomas Edison fell into a grain elevator, like the one pictured, while trying to see inside it.

school. He did not like math and his constant questions made his teacher angry. Once again, Thomas's curiosity got him into trouble. He was beaten for asking too many questions.

In addition to beating Thomas, his teacher called him stupid. His mother was so angry with his teacher that she decided to teach Thomas herself, and she took him out of school. Altogether, Thomas attended public school for about three months. Although he had little formal schooling, Thomas's parents made sure that he received a good education at home.

Home School

Both of his parents loved books and encouraged all of the Edison children to read literature. His father introduced Thomas to the writings of Thomas Paine and English scientist Michael Faraday. Thomas's mother encouraged him to read the works of William Shakespeare and Charles Dickens. Both parents read fine literature and history books to the children and made sure that the children had books to read by themselves. Thomas's mother tried to guide her youngest son's curiosity toward finding out how things worked and doing experiments rather than getting into trouble. She encouraged him to explore and learn about his surroundings. When Thomas was nine years old his mother gave him a science book filled with experiments. Before long, Thomas had performed every experiment in the book. When his mother discovered how much he liked doing experiments, she bought him some more science books.

Nancy Edison taught her son at home. With her encouragement, Thomas explored the world of science and nature.

"My mother was the making of me," he said some years later. "She understood me; she let me follow my bent."[1] His mother allowed him to explore his natural talents.

Samuel Edison recalled his famous son's childhood. "Thomas Alva never had any boyhood days, his early amusements were steam engines and mechanical forces."[2]

Thomas would walk to mills and factories near his home, study and sketch the machinery, and then come home and build working models of the machines he

Edison is pictured as a young man conducting science experiments in his lab.

had seen. He enjoyed working with his hands and building devices. In addition to building these models, Thomas also liked to perform scientific experiments.

He enjoyed experimenting so much that when he was ten years old, he built himself a laboratory in the basement of the family's home so he could experiment without making a mess in the house. After a year of experimenting with chemicals and building models of machinery, Thomas built a telegraph that really worked.

Some of Thomas's scientific experiments caused terrible odors to drift up from the basement into the house. Although Thomas bought some of the chemicals for his laboratory in town, some he found in the town dump, and he labeled all of his chemicals "poison" so no one would touch them.

Thomas's father was pleased that his son's curiosity led him to learn all he could about the world around him and how different machines worked. But Thomas's father did not care for Thomas's chemistry experiments. In fact, he bribed Thomas with pennies to experiment less and to read more books. Instead of reading more, Thomas used the pennies to buy more chemicals for his basement laboratory. But soon he would have far less time to spend in his home laboratory.

Odd Jobs

Because the family had money problems, Thomas looked for ways to help support his family. He and a boy named Michael Oates began raising fruits and vegetables. In their first summer harvest they made more than two hundred dollars. Thomas gave most of the money he made from selling his share of the produce to his family. But Thomas did not want to spend his time hoeing the garden in the hot sun, so he looked for other ways to make money.

At twelve, Thomas took a job as a candy seller on the Trunk Line Railroad. The train had a five-hour stop in Detroit, Michigan. Thomas used that time to explore the city. When he located the library, he knew he had found a useful way to spend his spare time. Thomas spent hours reading about subjects that interested him. It was rumored that he read every book in the library.

As with his garden, he gave much of the money he earned working on the Trunk Line Railroad to his parents. The rest he spent on chemicals and books. But doing one thing at a time was never enough for Thomas, so soon he was looking for more ways to make money.

The Newspaper Business

He used part of his earnings to buy an old printing press. He set up the press in a baggage car on the train, and he was soon selling newspapers to passengers on the train and to the people at the train stops. Thomas was the reporter, the editor, and the printer. He named his one-page newspaper the *Weekly Herald.* He even sold ads to restaurants and hotels along the train's route. Newspapers helped Thomas earn a lot of money.

When Thomas was fourteen years old, the Civil War broke out between the northern and the southern states. Although some boys near Thomas's age were signing up with the army, Thomas could not. He had a hearing problem, which began when he was a small child and had grown steadily worse. This hearing problem kept him from becoming a soldier. So Thomas remained with the Trunk Line Railroad and kept printing and selling his papers. It was one of the battles of the Civil War that gave Thomas the idea for one of his best money-making opportunities.

At age twelve, Thomas wrote, edited, and sold copies of his newspaper, the *Weekly Herald*, to train passengers.

People were very interested in news of the battles. On an April day in 1862, the *Detroit Free Press* learned of the Battle of Shiloh, a battle that took place in Tennessee. Thomas was at the newspaper's office picking up some of their papers to sell and saw the story before the paper was printed. He talked the **telegrapher** in Detroit into

Thomas earned money by selling newspapers carrying early accounts of the Battle of Shiloh (pictured).

sending a message to all of the train stops along the route that the train would carry newspapers with information about the battle. At the first stop, where a small crowd of people waited for the news, he charged a nickel for each copy of the paper. Farther down the line the crowds were larger and Thomas charged a dime, then fifteen cents. By the time Thomas and the train reached the end of the line, he was selling the paper for thirty-five cents a copy. Thomas made a lot of money. He also learned the importance of the telegraph, and would soon learn to become a telegraph operator, his first real adult job.

Chapter Two

A Rocky Road to Discovery

One summer day as sixteen-year-old Thomas carried his newspapers to the train, he saw a small child crawling on the tracks in front of a moving boxcar. Thomas dropped his papers, dashed to the tracks, and snatched the child from the path of the train. The child was the son of Mount Clemens telegrapher J.U. Mackenzie. Mackenzie was so grateful for his son's safety that he offered Thomas anything that was in his power to give. Thomas wanted to learn to be a telegrapher—a person who uses Morse code to send and receive messages—and so Mackenzie granted Thomas's wish and taught him the telegrapher's trade.

Edison the Tramp Telegrapher

By age seventeen, Edison was a traveling telegrapher, also called a tramp telegrapher. He enjoyed the freedom of traveling to different parts of the United States, and he even worked for a time in Canada.

He liked working at night so he could have the daylight hours for his experiments. But sometimes working all night long and experimenting all day got him into trouble. While working a night shift at Stratford Junction in Ontario, Canada, Edison's job was to warn train stations about trains traveling in both directions through Stratford Junction. He was supposed to prove he was staying awake through his night shift by telegraphing a message to the nearest dispatcher every thirty minutes. Edison thought this time was better spent napping, and so he made a device that would automatically send a signal every thirty minutes. One

Even after he became a famous inventor Edison sometimes slept on the job.

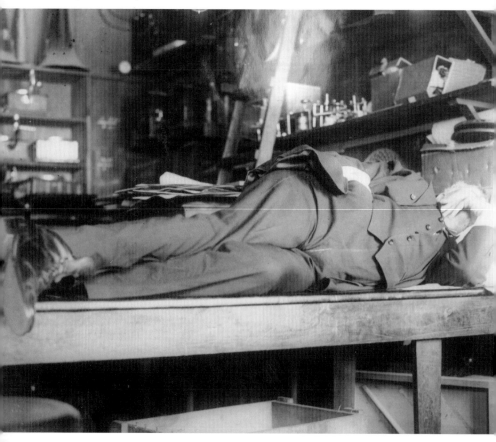

night the dispatcher became suspicious and sent Edison an extra message. Edison was asleep at the time and did not answer the dispatcher's message. The dispatcher sent an assistant to check Edison's junction station. The assistant caught Edison sleeping. Edison was fired.

At least for a while, he learned his lesson about sleeping on the job, but at another Canadian station he accidentally missed the signal of an oncoming train. The engineer in the approaching train, not knowing that there was a train on the tracks, was barreling straight toward him. Luckily, each engineer saw the other's lights, and the trains were able to stop just in time to avoid a terrible accident. Edison was so afraid he might be arrested for his carelessness that he left Canada immediately and returned to the United States. But Edison's problems did not end when he left Canada.

Because he was so often distracted from his job by his experiments and inventions, and because he sometimes used his employers' equipment to perform his experiments, he did not last very long at any telegrapher's job. His average time at a station was about six months.

Traveling Tom

He could usually get another telegrapher's job, but during especially hard times he had to take whatever work he could find. Once, times were so bad that Edison had to work on a railroad gang, helping build bridges across an Arkansas river. Another time he found himself in New Orleans stranded without a job.

During his travels, Edison took a job building a railway bridge in Arkansas, like the one shown here.

By then he had been on the road for nearly six years and was terribly homesick. He used the last of his money to travel home to Port Huron, Michigan. His days as a tramp telegrapher had come to an end but a new stage in his life was about to begin.

A New Beginning in Boston

Although Edison was glad to see his family again, he knew he would not stay long in Port Huron. He needed a job.

His friend, Milton Adams, had gone to work for the Western Union Telegraph Company in Boston, Massachusetts. Edison wrote to Adams, asking if the

Boston office might have a job for him. Adams wrote back with good news of a job opening.

Edison's new job was to send telegraph messages to New York City. He soon proved himself to be the fastest telegraph operator in Boston. Because the Boston and New York offices were rivals, a contest was held between Edison and New York's best telegrapher to see who was fastest. Edison won.

Although Edison continued to experiment and invent, he did not allow his experimenting to cost him his job. He remained with the Boston Western Union office for nearly a year.

In Boston he found a bookshop that carried books of experiments by one of his favorite scientists,

The offices of Western Union, where Edison became the fastest telegraph operator in Boston.

Michael Faraday. "I think I must have tried about everything in those books,"[3] he said later.

It seems appropriate that one of Edison's first inventions would keep track of the price of gold. The stock ticker automatically received information about current prices of gold from the Boston Gold Exchange. This information was sent from one machine to another in much the same way telegraphers sent messages over wires.

By then, Edison had given up his telegrapher's job and was working as a full-time inventor. He rented thirty of the stock tickers to businesspeople, but after paying some of his debts, he was almost out of money. He was also ready to make another move.

Edison invented the stock ticker, which kept track of gold prices.

An Inventor on the Move

Edison took a big chance by moving to New York City. He had little money and no job or friends waiting for him there. But when he arrived, he did what he did best: He used his wits. While walking down a city street, hungry and thirsty, he saw a teashop. He entered the shop and asked the owner if he would like to have his teas judged to see which was the best. The owner thought this was a good idea, and he let Edison sample the teas.

Edison had no place to live, but as he made the rounds of companies that might need a man with his skills, he met Franklin L. Pope, an electrical engineer with the Gold Indicator Company. Although Pope could not give Edison a job, he allowed Edison to sleep on a cot in his office. One day the main machine, which the entire office depended on for transmitting gold prices to all of its customers, stopped. The office panicked. Edison found a broken wire deep inside the machine and repaired it. He was given a job and paid three hundred dollars a month, a huge salary at that time.

Now Edison had a job and a place to live. He could have spent his money on nice clothes, fine furniture, and fancy restaurants, but he chose to save his money, and before long he was able to set up his own laboratory in Newark, New Jersey, and work full time on his experiments. Franklin Pope, the man who gave him a place to sleep, became one of his partners. One of Edison's new inventions was an improved stock ticker, which he sold to Marshall Lefferts, the president of the Gold and Stock Company, for $40,000. With this money, he was able to expand his lab.

In 1871, after the New Jersey lab had been open for several years, Edison married Mary Stillwell on Christmas day. It was rumored that Edison, always the inventor, spent part of his wedding day in the laboratory, leaving his new bride home alone.

After a while, Edison wanted a quieter place to work and to think. Soon Edison, now with a family, would make another move.

Chapter Three

The Menlo Park Days

Although his years in Newark were happy and productive, Edison wanted to find a new site for his lab. He felt the city was noisy and distracted him and his workers from their tasks. He also needed more room to work. Because Edison was busy most of the time, he asked his father to help him find the new site. Samuel Edison found a place called Menlo Park, a small New Jersey town about twenty-four miles from New York City.

The World's First Invention Factory

The Menlo Park "invention factory" was made up of several buildings. Edison's library and office were in a two-story brick building. The laboratory was a long, wooden two-story building. The Edisons' family home was nearby, so Edison had only a short walk to work. Several outbuildings stood on the property.

Edison hired the best scientists and engineers to work at the Menlo Park invention factory and at times had sixty people working on inventions in the laboratory.

Edison invented important things at this Menlo Park lab such as the light bulb and the phonograph.

Edison set goals, both for himself and for his staff. He expected to produce one minor invention every ten days and a major invention every six months. To do this, Edison and his staff worked long hours. Eighty-hour work weeks were not unusual, and sometimes he would push his staff to work around the clock, twenty-four hours or more, without any time away from the lab.

Although the Menlo Park staff worked long, hard hours, they also had time for fun. They would take a break around midnight, have a light meal, sing, and dance. This work environment proved successful because from this small New Jersey town came inventions that changed the world.

Menlo Park Inventions

Just after moving to Menlo Park, Edison went to work on ways to improve an existing invention, Alexander Graham Bell's telephone. Bell's telephone could carry spoken messages only a few miles. Edison felt that he could create a better telephone. The telephone developed at Menlo Park could carry voices great distances, and the voices could be heard more clearly. Edison's improvements to the telephone earned him a quarter of a million dollars.

His work on the telephone started Edison thinking about ways to record the human voice. He developed a device called a phonograph. A phonograph is a machine with a rotating cylinder, a needle, and a **diaphragm**. The diaphragm would "catch" sound waves and the attached needle would etch grooves, caused by

Edison's first phonograph. He was surprised to find that it really worked.

the movement of the diaphragm, into the rotating cylinder. The sounds recorded on the cylinder could then be played back by placing the needle in the groove, rotating the cylinder, and amplifying the sound waves caused by the vibrations of the needle through a conelike device called a horned speaker. As they worked on this invention, one of Edison's assistants bet Edison two dollars that the invention would never work. Edison was confident he could reproduce the sounds of voices and music. When Edison recorded and played back the nursery rhyme "Mary Had a Little Lamb," his assistant had to pay off the bet. But Edison was shocked that it had worked so easily.

"I was never so taken aback in all my life. I was always afraid of things that worked the first time,"[4] he said.

The Birth of the Light Bulb

Developing the electric light, however, was not so simple. In later years, Edison spoke of those days at Menlo Park. "The electric light has caused me the greatest amount of study and has required the most elaborate experiments."[5]

The Menlo Park laboratory was kept busy for hundreds of hours creating a light bulb that would produce light for longer than a few minutes. Edison knew that for an electric light bulb to be useful and practical, it would have to burn for many hours, not just a few minutes.

He had to find something to use as a **filament**, the material in a light bulb that glows. Edison tried hundreds of materials as filaments, including human hair

Edison's first light bulb (right). Edison is shown in his lab experimenting with filament materials that could best conduct light.

and horsehair. He sent people throughout the world in search of different kinds of materials to use. He discovered that long, thin filaments lasted longer than short, thick ones. He also discovered that plant fiber made the best filaments.

To keep the filaments from burning up, they had to be in a **vacuum**, a space without air. Edison had glass blowers make small globes. He pumped the air out of the globe and ran an electrical current from a **generator** through a wire in the globe's base. This caused the filament to glow. Edison and his staff watched one light bulb glow for forty hours. He knew he had a success.

Edison's years at Menlo Park were even more productive than his years at Newark, New Jersey, but he and his family would soon experience a sad and difficult time.

Home and Family

By 1878 Thomas and Mary Edison had three children, Marion Estelle, Thomas Alva Jr., and William Leslie. Edison nicknamed his oldest two children "Dot" and "Dash" in honor of his work on the telegraph. Although Edison was away from his family for days at a time while working in the laboratory, he enjoyed spending time with his wife and playing games with their children.

Mary was quiet, shy, and often lonely. She did not like to be in large crowds of people. She talked her sister, Alice Stillwell, into living with her for a time and keeping her company. But eventually Alice married and went to live in her own home.

But the Menlo Park days came to an end in 1884. Mary Edison developed **typhoid fever** and died on

Pictured are Mary Edison and Thomas Alva Jr.

August 9, at the age of twenty-nine. Edison was so grief stricken that he could no longer bear to work in the lab. Because Menlo Park held too many memories of his beloved Mary, he and his children moved to New York City. He seldom returned to Menlo Park. Sadly, another chapter had closed in Edison's life. But little did he know how soon the next chapter would begin.

Chapter Four

West Orange, New Jersey

W hen Edison arrived in New York City, a widowed, thirty-seven-year-old father with three children, he was depressed and heartbroken. He fought his loneliness the only way he knew how: He threw himself into his work to try to forget his grief. But in a few months' time, he found happiness again.

A New Wife; a New Beginning

Six months after his wife's death, Edison was visiting in the home of a friend. Also visiting that evening was eighteen-year-old Mina Miller. Edison was attracted to her immediately, but for most of the next few months Edison and Mina were in different cities, so what little time they had together was important to both of them. Then one day Edison taught Mina Morse code. Once she learned the code, he tapped out a message for her. It was a marriage proposal. They were married in February 1886.

Mina was just the opposite of Mary. Instead of being shy, she was outgoing. She was raised in a well-to-do family and was not uncomfortable at the social events the wife of a famous inventor had to attend with her husband. After the marriage, Mina's first job was to win over Edison's children. Naturally, the older children resented someone taking their mother's place. But with a great deal of patience, Mina was able to unite the family.

The Edisons found a new home, Glenmont, a twenty-three room house near West Orange, New Jersey. The house was so large that it took a staff of twelve servants to take care of it. But it was not just the mansion that brought Edison to West Orange. West Orange was also the site of his new laboratory.

The Edisons' new home, Glenmont, was a twenty-three-room mansion staffed with a dozen servants.

Highlights of the West Orange Laboratory

Edison's new invention factory was even bigger and better than Menlo Park. Once again, he pushed himself and his workers round the clock to complete projects. But he also hosted parties and picnics to entertain his workers and their families. There was usually a baseball game at the picnics, and Edison liked to be on hand to throw out the first ball.

One of the most important projects to come out of the West Orange laboratory was the motion picture. In Edison's words, "I am experimenting upon an instrument which does for the eye what the phonograph does for the ear."[6]

Edison had been successful in recording sound when he created the phonograph. Now he wanted to record movement. Edison and his assistant, William Kennedy-Laurie Dickson, developed a device called a **kinetograph**. The kinetograph was a box with a lens that held a strip of a new type of photographic film developed by George Eastman. An electric motor moved the film, photographing a sequence of pictures. After developing the film, it was viewed in a **kinetoscope**, a cabinet with a peep hole and an electric motor. When the sprocket wheels turned, the images on the strip of developed film appeared to move. Edison **patented** the kinetograph and the kinetoscope in 1888.

Edison could see a future for his moving pictures, and in 1893 he built the Black Maria, the world's first motion picture studio. It was a long black box of a room, fifty feet long. The entire room was mounted on

A photographer displays Edison's kinetograph camera which made moving pictures.

a base that would allow it to swing around to follow the position of the sun. It was terribly hot and uncomfortable for the technicians and the people being filmed.

Edison continued to work with motion pictures and, in 1903, The Edison Manufacturing Company released the black-and-white film, *The Great Train Robbery,* which became America's first great box-office hit. The movie was on one reel and told an entire story in fourteen scenes. It was only ten minutes long. In addition to his other experiments and inventions, Edison continued to work with his moving pictures and, in 1912, he combined the phonograph and the kinetograph to make the first "talking pictures."

Later Years

Another invention Edison worked to improve at West Orange was a storage battery that could be recharged. The United States, fearing it would soon become involved in

A scene from *The Great Train Robbery,* a film released by the Edison Manufacturing Company in 1903.

World War I, had placed his storage batteries on a new experimental submarine. The submarine had an explosion, killing five sailors. Although some important safety rules had not been followed, the batteries were blamed. But despite the accident, the U.S. government wanted to use Edison's skills in the war effort. In 1915 at the age of sixty-eight, Edison was named president of the Naval Advisory Board. One of his duties was to help plan a research lab, modeled after his own lab at West Orange. Edison was disappointed that all the research lab was allowed to work on was submarine-detecting devices. He felt that the government-chosen people running the lab were unimaginative and short-sighted. He preferred the creative environment of West Orange.

A Busy Retirement

By 1920 the West Orange lab had more than ten thousand employees. It was a bustling place similar to today's research and development labs. Edison knew it was time to put the management of the lab into younger hands, so in 1926 he turned over control of the West Orange lab to his son Charles, one of Edison's three children by his second wife, Mina. But Edison's productive days were far from over. He had built another lab at his winter home in Fort Meyers, Florida. One project of the Fort Meyers lab was finding ways to make rubber from plants so that the United States would not have to import rubber from other countries. He had hundreds of kinds of trees and shrubs brought to the lab to be tested, and he was able to produce a high grade of rubber from the goldenrod plant.

Edison's health began to fail, but for a while he was able to enjoy the fruits of his lifetime's work. One of Edison's earlier employees, Henry Ford, the creator of

Automobile assembly line inventor Henry Ford (left) was once employed by Thomas Edison (right).

the Ford automobile, bought the old Menlo Park lab, including seven carloads of topsoil and all of the original equipment. He had it moved from New Jersey and restored on the grounds of Ford's museum, Greenfield Village, at Dearborn, Michigan, near the Ford automobile plant. In October 1929, Ford brought his old mentor to the reconstructed lab and walked him through it. Edison commented, "We never kept it as clean as this!"[7]

A replica of Edison's laboratory at the Ford Museum in Dearborn, Michigan.

Later that same day, during a banquet in his honor, Edison became ill and had to leave. Although he continued to stay busy, his health grew worse over the next two years until, in September 1931, he fell into a coma. Thomas Alva Edison died on October 18, 1931. The evening of his death, people all across America turned off their lights for one minute in his honor. Even the lights surrounding the Statue of Liberty were turned off. His body lay in state in the West Orange lab for two days and he was buried at nearby Roosevelt Cemetery. Later, his body was moved to the grounds of the Edison estate at Glenmont, where he was buried next to Mina's grave.

Throughout his lifetime, Edison patented more than one thousand inventions. Although he was liked by some and envied by others, no one can deny that Thomas Edison forever changed the way we live.

Notes

Chapter 1: Curious Al

1. Quoted in Matthew Josephson, *Edison: A Biography.* New York: John Wiley & Sons, 1992, p. 22.
2. Quoted in Josephson, *Edison,* p. 23.

Chapter 2: A Rocky Road to Discovery

3. Quoted in Martin Melosi, *Thomas Alva Edison and the Modernization of America.* New York: Harper-Collins, 1990, p. 26.

Chapter 3: The Menlo Park Days

4. Quoted in Gene Adair, *Thomas Alva Edison: Inventing the Electronic Age.* New York: Oxford University Press, 1996, p. 62.
5. Quoted in Adair, *Thomas Alva Edison,* p. 71.

Chapter 4: West Orange, New Jersey

6. Quoted in Neil Baldwin, *Edison: Inventing the Century.* New York: Hyperion, 1995, p. 211.
7. Quoted in Adair, *Thomas Alva Edison,* p. 125.

Glossary

diaphragm: A thin flexible disc that vibrates when struck by sound waves.

filament: A long, thin flexible wire or fiber; the glowing wire in a light bulb.

generator: A machine that can change mechanical energy into electrical energy.

kinetograph: A device that takes a series of photographs of moving objects.

kinetoscope: A device used to view a series of pictures through a magnifying lens.

patent: A document that gives an inventor total control over an invention for a period of years.

telegrapher: A person who sends and receives telegraph messages using a system of dots and dashes called Morse code.

typhoid fever: A life-threatening illness caused by the spread of a certain type of bacteria found in contaminated water or food.

vacuum: A space, such as a glass globe, from which air has been removed.

For Further Exploration

David A. Adler, *Thomas Alva Edison: Great Inventor.* New York: Holiday House, 1990. An interesting narrative of the productive life of Thomas Alva Edison, detailing both his successes and failures. Heavily illustrated in black and white.

Vincent Buranelli, *Thomas Alva Edison.* Englewood Cliffs, NJ: Silver Burdett Press, 1989. A well-detailed account of the personal and professional life of the inventor.

Christopher Lampton, *Thomas Alva Edison.* Lakeville, CT: Grey Castle Press, 1981. A fairly detailed narrative of the mischievous childhood, trouble-plagued early career, failures, tragedies, and successes of Thomas Alva Edison.

Nina Morgan, *Thomas Edison.* New York: The Bookwright Press, 1991. A well-written biography with many colorful illustrations and diagrams.

Robert Quackenbush, *What Has Wild Tom Done Now?!!* Englewood Cliffs, NJ: Prentice-Hall, 1980. A sometimes humorous account of the adventures and misadventures of Thomas Alva Edison.

Theodore Roland-Entwhistle, *Thomas Edison.* New York: Marshall Cavendish, 1988. A fast-paced biography. The colorful illustrations and sidebars add drama and detail to the text.

Index

Picture Credits

About the Author

Sheila Wyborny lives in Houston, Texas, with her husband, Wendell. They like to spend their free time flying their Cessna aircraft and looking for antiques to add to their small collection.